FAMILY

A CHURCH CHALLENGE FOR THE 80s

DOLORES CURRAN

Copyright © 1980 by the National Conference of Diocesan Directors of Religious Education—CCD

Library of Congress Catalog Card Number: 80-50480

ISBN: 0-86683-640-3 (previously ISBN 0-03-057549)

Winston Press, Inc.
430 Oak Grove
Minneapolis, Minnesota 55403

5 4 3 2

Contents

Foreword

The calendar year 1980 carries with it strong significance for many sectors of our contemporary society. It is the beginning of another new year, it bears the full impact of the whole new decade, it institutes the final fifth of the century, and it challenges us to revel in fantasy and fact about what lies ahead for us in this new era of the 80s.

In Catholic Church circles 1980 has been designated by the U.S. Bishops as the Year of the Family and the 80s as the Decade of the Family. This emphasis found its origin in stated priorities listed by the U.S. Bishops, namely Parish Renewal, Evangelization, and Family Ministry. Accordingly, a Pastoral Plan for Family Ministry was developed by the staff of the Department of Education at the United States Catholic Conference, which was intended to be used by dioceses throughout the country in order to surface needs and construct positive programmatic responses to the various critical pastoral areas of the American family today. Appropriate resource material were developed in 1978 and 1979 in order to facilitate a proper and well-grounded approach to these concerns.

In 1978 the National Conference of Diocesan Directors of Religious Education—CCD, better known as NCDD, surveyed its membership for an appropriate topic for its 1979 Resource Paper. One of the two topics emerging from such a listing was a great concern for the rising phenomenon within catechetical circles known as family catechesis. There seemed to be a great and immediate need for information and clarification as to what such a term really means, where such programs are happening, what models are working, what direction is to be taken, upon what foundations such a creative approach is to be built, and what resources are available.

The Executive Committee of NCDD commissioned such a paper to be written, and Dolores Curran of Littleton, Colorado was the obvious choice to be its author.

She brings to this particular project a reputation as an expert in this area based on her experience in writing, lecturing, raising a family, and involvement in parish catechetical programs. She is nationally known as an author of many books and articles in catechetics as well as for her syndicated column "Talks with Parents." She is in demand as a convention speaker and workshop presenter. She has served on many Church commissions and was a delegate to the Call to Action Gathering in Detroit in 1976 as well as a member of the Family Life Commission. She is preeminently qualified for such a work as the 1979 NCDD Resource Paper.

After much deliberation, this book bears the title *Family: A Church Challenge for the 80s.* The author touches on such basic foundational cornerstones as the statement from the documents of Vatican II in the 60s, which state that parents are the primary teachers of their children in matters of religion, to the thrust of the National Catechetical Directory in the 70s, which seeks to establish the fundamental role of the family and the community in the catechetical process. Curran engages her expertise and her experience to set forth the challenge and vision to lead catechists, administrators, parents, clergy, and readers in general into the 80s, the Decade of the Family.

The following pages stress the author's research and perspective on the nature of family catechetics and how it really works in today's shifting sociological scene. Curran investigates the needs of the contemporary Catholic family and how to respond to such needs, and she offers models of existing programs in the ever increasing programmatic thrust called family catechetics. Finally, in a spirit of hope for the future, Curran calls for and challenges all to a shared pastoral vision and an integrated catechetical ministry for parishes and dioceses throughout the country.

The NCDD is most grateful for the work and words of Dolores Curran and her challenging contribution to the contemporary catechetical scene. The NCDD is equally appreciative to Winston Press for publishing this book which will provide a viable resource to workers in the catechetical field.

Challenge, hope, vision, models, ideas, needs and plans, theory and practice, dreams and realities, each idea is presented in a creative and challenging way to urge all of us to cooperate with the Spirit in finding better and more effective ways to share the light of faith in a family context.

Rev. David E. Beebe, Executive Secretary, NCDD

Introduction

We need continually to reevaluate our Church programs in light of changing needs, examining our whole educational apostolate to see that it has the proper relationship of family, church, and community. We need to work without ceasing to uphold the principle that parents have the basic responsibility for the education of their children. At the same time we must give them the support they need to do an effective job of giving to the generation to come the unchanging values of the life of faith.[1]

Archbishop Peter L. Gerety

No matter how you read the statistics on marriage and family life today you cannot overlook the fact that there is trouble in this basic unit of ecclesial and civil society and that even good families and better than average married couples are in need of extra support. In a word, they are in need of the specialized concern of a ministry which will deal with them in terms of all the facets of church life—educationally, liturgically, socially.[2]

Father Donald Conroy
Family Life Representative
United States Catholic Conference

There's some in my parish concerned about what their children aren't learning, but I can't get too worried about basics and all that when our boy hasn't spoken to anyone in the family for three weeks.

Parent
Call to Action Hearing, 1975

Returning to the basics seems to be a panacea today for many of the ills of family and society. It is most loudly touted in education and in religious education, often, paradoxically, by those least able to define the basics they espouse. The more educated the parent, the less likely he or she is to support a return to the fundamental-school concept. The more faith-rounded the Catholic parent, the less likely he or she is to accept memorization of content as evidence of successful religious education. Still, a call for a return to the basics echoes in our Church.

In each of the introductory quotes, some form of *basic* is used but with a wide range in meaning. Archbishop Gerety speaks of the *basic* responsibility of parents, and Father Conroy of the family as the *basic* unit of Church and civil society; the parent calling for help in learning how to communicate with her teenage son, uses the more popular reference to the *basics* as a body of knowledge which many of today's parents in our Church equate with faith. If asked to define those basics, most parents list the Ten Commandments, Church laws, and other content. They fail to include themselves. Yet, both religious educators and empirical data convince us that parents are the most important determinant in a person's lifelong faith. One family catechist, Sister Sandra DeGidio, OSM, refers to parents as the real basics in a child's religious education and describes the parish's role as supportive of the parental mission:

> The basics we need to return to are that parents are not only the primary, but the best teachers of their children in terms of faith and religious and moral growth and development. . . . The parish's greatest contribution to families is through its work with parents. Aiding them in their growth, affirming and supporting them in their role as parents and transmitters of faith is our most important task in the designing and implementing of family programs. If parents are secure in their faith, if we help them to live that faith life, to ritualize it, to be aware of the numerous teachable moments they have every day, the faith will indeed be passed on to the next generation.[3]

In those words we hear echoes of the Second Vatican Council which declared that parents are "the first and foremost educators of their children" and that "their role as educators is so decisive that scarcely anything can compensate for their failure in it."[4]

Yet, we find that most of our cathechetical efforts, short of sacramental preparation, attempt to compensate for parental apathy, lack of confidence, and general willingness to turn over the responsibility for their children's faith to other parish personnel. Even the most committed DRE, the most visionary pastoral team, and the most persevering idealist can age into crusty cynicism after a few years of focusing on family-centered catechesis. Puzzled by parents who claim they want religion for their children but steadfastly refuse to value themselves as instrumental in that goal, frustrated by demands for ever broadening ministry to the family and to that family-of-families, the parish, and constantly taken to task by sociologists and religious theorists for their failures to create viable faith communities within families, these diocesan and parish practitioners are likely to give up in despair. Their loss is costly, because these are the very personnel we most need to hear, to affirm, and to support. They are heralds of the future at a time when many in our pews and in our leadership are advocating a return to the past. John Westerhoff III attributes this perspective to confusion:

> Everyone seems to want some change, but most are looking backward for insight at present. There is a lot of confusion in people's minds about their faith, and they are groping. They wish God was more real and life was more meaningful.[5]

Why is family-centered catechesis so easy to espouse in document but so difficult to achieve in parishes? Why are those most capable of showing us the way to parish renewal and evangelization through the family least supported? Where are the models of successful family-centered programs? What makes up the family? What constitutes family catechesis? What are the major reasons for success or failure in family-centered programs? These are a few of the questions I hope to address in this paper. My underlying goal is to write frankly of the needs in the real family, not the mythical "good Catholic family" of old, to survey what is and what is not working in the area of family-centered catechesis and why, and to suggest action, coordination, and support for workable and viable family catechesis in a variety of parish settings. To reach this goal, I am depending heavily on information from countless authorities in the field of family. To them, many of whom are counted in the rosters of the NCDD, we are all indebted.

For those to whom such things are important, some author background is in order. My interest in family-centered catechesis evolves from a triple thrust: education, writing, and family. I have published six books on various phases of family and religion. I write a weekly column, "Talks With Parents," which goes into over 3 million homes and draws nearly 100 letters weekly from parents around the country. From these letters, I keep my finger on the Catholic family pulse today (at least the churched pulse). I find that parents tend to view a family columnist as a surrogate Church person, one to whom they can divulge deep feelings (without admitting to Father or Sister), changing value systems, or their failures as Catholic parents.

Equally important has been my work on various commissions within the Church. These have helped me to view family from the perspective of the professional as well. Commissions pertinent to this paper include four: The Family Writing Committee of the Call to Action; the Ad Hoc Commission on Marriage and Family, which drew up the Pastoral Plan for Family Ministry; the USCC Symposium on Youth and Catechesis; and the Parenting Guidelines Committee. My association with diocesan directors as a result of consulting with them on family programs or speaking at diocesan catechetical congresses has been immensely educational in viewing family and Church from that perspective. Finally, I am the parent of three, including two teenagers.

A brief overview of recent history and efforts in family-centered catechesis might be helpful here. In our eagerness to flesh out our vision with immediate results, it is wise to remember that actual efforts in the field are less than ten years old, a mere page in the annals of religious education. In 1967, as columnist for *The Parent Educator,* a now defunct magazine published a decade before its time, by Neil Kluepfel of Twenty-Third Publications, I was invited to be part of a panel on family religion at a large diocesan religious education congress. There were three of us on the panel and seventeen in the audience. Ten years later, I was invited to address an adjoining diocesan congress focusing on family, and I spoke to three thousand. Within the past ten years the major religious education congresses have chosen family as their annual theme. In ten years we have seen the growth of family personnel on a diocesan level, the appearance of numerous programs, series, and films on family by major religious publishers, summer workshops devoted to family education, and measurable efforts in nearly every diocese in the country.

Emphasis on family catechesis was reborn with Vatican Council II and has been stressed as a primary method of transmitting the faith by every major document since then: *The General Catechetical Directory, To Teach as Jesus Did,* and *The National Catechetical Directory.* Ministry to and by the family has been chosen by our own Bishops' Conference as a ten-year thrust beginning with the Year of the Family in 1980.

Historically, the idea of family as the central vehicle of transmitting faith is unassailable. H. I. Marrou writes:

> Christian education of children, through which they learnt to share in the treasury of the faith, to submit to a healthy discipline in the matter of morals, was the parents' fundamental duty. There was more in this than was contained in the Roman tradition: it was essentially a continuation of the Jewish tradition, which emphasized the importance of the family in the development of religious consciousness. And this duty could not be delegated; the early Church would have had sharp words to say about "Christian" parents of today who think that they have done all that is required of them when they have passed their children over to a teacher or an institution.[6]

In ideal, then, we have moved from a child- and content-centered catechesis to a family-centered catechesis, while in practice we remain primarily child- and content-centered. However, it is important to remember that every major educational change begins with the ideal and moves gradually out of the old pattern. This is not to say that every educational innovation becomes accepted, but that it takes considerably longer than one decade to move from document to reality in our Church. This is borne out in this sobering passage from the National Inventory of Parish Catechetical Programs conducted by the USCC and Catholic University:

> When one reviews recent studies such as those by Urie Bronfenbrenner or reads the recent Carnegie study *All Our Children* and *The National Catechetical Directory,* no doubt is left about the need for family ministry. Personnel must be found and materials produced that respond to the need. In light of the fact, however, that approximately one-half of the

nation's parishes will not or cannot budget a salary for DREs and that, after almost ten years, half of the nation's DREs report they have no role description, many questions are raised about the future survival of family ministry.[7]

Still, as slowly as the adoption of family-centered catechesis seems to be moving, there is no doubt that it is moving. However, family-centered catechesis is likely to be hastened more by a better understanding of the rationale behind it and by visible models of success than by statements and pleas.

* * * * *

Definitions of terminology are always a regrettable necessity in papers like this, regrettable because it seems so simplistic yet necessary to assure ourselves that we are talking about the same people, goals, and challenges. The terms I will discuss here are *family, religious education,* and *catechesis.*

After wrestling with the definition of *family* on three commissions the past few years, I realize that I could inundate readers with pages of definitions and still not find a consensus. From the definition of *family* used by the Census Bureau, "a group of people related by blood, marriage, or adoption living under the same roof," to the literary, "two or more people sharing a history and a future," to the bald all-inclusive definition, "folks," I will opt toward the last. Perhaps it is more effective to explain what my definition is not. When I use the word *family,* I am not using the usual parish definition—a couple and their school-aged children. Rather, I include all those who were or are members of a family of some kind—single parents, widowed, committed singles, children, couples, teens, and handicapped. I also include hurting families, unchurched families, and those that Joseph Iannone refers to as the underchurched families. When I talk about family-centered catechesis, then, I include all those who view themselves as actual or potential members of the parish family. Committed singles and widowed people living alone are a family unto themselves. They have much to share with coupled families and youth. The parish is a family of families. No one should be excluded from parish family ministry because he or she has no school-aged children. One widowed grandmother stated her role beautifully for us at a parenting workshop, "I am a resource person for my grandchildren." In a viable parish family ministry, she would also be a resource person for her peers, her pew mates, and other people's grandchildren. She is what Maureen Gallagher, chief author of Paulist's *Family,* refers to as a sage, one of the four categories of catechist in the early church.

Stickier to define but equally necessary is the difference between *religious education* and *catechesis.* I wish to use the distinction Barard Marthaler made in *Catechetics in Context* (Huntington, IN: Our Sunday Visitor, 1973), page 35:

> Religious education and catechesis are not synonymous. Berard Marthaler is correct when he suggests that religious education is primarily an academic enterprise whether in the context of school or not, while catechesis is essentially a pastoral activity, an activity intended to transmit the church's faith and to aid that faith to become living, conscious and active in the life of maturing persons and a maturing community.

Using this definition, religious education concentrates more on the content or message that is passed on than on the total faith life of a person. In *To Teach as Jesus Did* we are called to focus, not on message alone, but on community and service as well. Westerhoff, in his incisive book, *Will Our Children Have Faith?*, draws a strong distinction between religion and faith:

> You can teach about religion, but you cannot teach people faith. . . . It appears that as Christian faith has diminished, the schooling-instructional paradigm has encouraged us to busy ourselves with teaching about Christian religion. As our personal commitment to Christ has lapsed, many church persons have turned for solace to teaching children what the Bible says, what happened in the history of the church, what we believe, and what is right and wrong. . . . For many today, Christian religion as taught in our church schools stands between them and God. The schooling-instruction paradigm easily leads us into thinking that we have done our jobs if we teach children all *about* Christianity.[8]

The use of *catechesis* in this paper, then, will include all those elements that contribute to a living faith, including but not limited to message, content, and doctrine.

1 Analysis of NCDD Requests of This Paper

The process by which this paper was developed was set up by the Executive Committee of the National Conference of Diocesan Directors (NCDD) to direct the author to focus on actual concerns and interests of members in the area of family. To accomplish this goal, diocesan directors were asked to submit responses to two questions: "Do you have any specific concerns in this area (of family catechesis) that you would like to see addressed in this paper?" and "Do you have any directions for the author?" About sixty responses were returned, but many of these represented offices of religious education or other groups in dioceses, so approximately eighty respondents voiced their concerns and hopes.

The great diversity in response revealed some interesting facts about diocesan directors themselves and about their perception of family as a catechetical endeavor. These four stand out:

Clear perception of the changing family in America. The catechists responding showed a realistic understanding of family today, particularly in the area of fragmentation—divorce, single parenting, and communication. Although some sociology will be necessary later on in the paper, response indicates that catechists are already aware of changing sociology to the degree that they don't have to be sold on needs. This is a very positive factor, because it indicates that they are sincerely interested in the faith life of a plurality of families, not just those who represent the intact, active, and supportive families in the parish.

Apparent confusion regarding purposes and goals of family-centered catechesis. This factor is less encouraging. While many directors flatly stated, "What we don't want is a listing of programs or new ways of getting families to teach religion," many others called for "evaluations of sacramental preparation programs" and "listing successful ways of getting parents to meetings." Some directors showed keen vision in seeing as the ultimate goal a renewed and living faith within the family which would turn outward in ministry to others. Other directors called for better ways of getting the family to teach the message. One respondent even used the phrase, "the family as mini-classroom." I hope this paper helps to clarify some of those differences.

Lack of reference to recent family developments in the Church. Only two directors mentioned the 1976 Call to Action Consultation in which families told us of their needs. Only two others asked for help in defining their role as catechists in the Plan of Pastoral Action for Family Ministry adopted by the bishops in May of 1978. Admittedly, this is a touchy area. It is under the auspices of the Family Life Office on the diocesan level, yet the most active and often the sole parish-level professional is the DRE. A great deal of cooperation and coordination will be necessary in implementing the Plan. Already, various diocesan personnel are finding overlaps in areas such as family faith enrichment, ministry to the divorced, and preparation of leadership couples. Struggles over budget, personnel, and authority are beginning to emerge. Diocesan directors rightfully resent being handed the responsibility for catechizing families under the Plan without being given decision-making powers and without being offered additional budget or personnel. I hear this resentment from education offices, but it did not surface on survey responses. Does this silence indicate lack of awareness of the Plan, or is it an effort to keep peace in offices where openness and cooperation must be achieved if the Plan is to succeed?

Need for additional research and papers on family. Again, the great diversity of requests of this paper indicate that directors are hungry for both research and practical papers on working with families. This paper, if it is to focus on family catechesis, can but touch on numerous areas requested by respondents. Other papers which might be indicated by requests include those on family sexuality, parish spiritual renewal, the intentionally extended family, the handicapped, intergenerational learning, communication skills within the family, interacting roles of the emerging laity/ declining clergy and religious, parent-teenage relationships, the relationship between culture and faith, ethnic traditions and values, and needs in the interfaith marriage.

2 Rationale Behind Family- Centered Catechesis

> We do not need to be convinced of the importance of the family. We know that. We know about family-centered religious education. We want to be challenged beyond that.
> Diocesan Director

While it is obvious that those at the level of leadership in diocesan offices and many of the parish DREs and religion teachers are convinced of the importance of the family, this conviction has not been successfully passed on to parishioners. One reason is that parishioners tend to see as valid only the methods by which they were taught religion, but another very real reason is the lack of convincing data imparted to them as evidence of their own importance in the faith process. They tend to attribute their importance to Father's or the DRE's opinion rather than to episcopal statements or hard data, or they attribute efforts to involve them to the shrinking supply of nuns available to really do the job properly. Many, of course, do not want to know their own importance, and we must confront that, too. Once when I gave a lecture on the importance of the father and offered data proving him to be the most important determinant in a child's faith, a father of five responded, "I don't want to hear about that. It's scary." The man sitting next to him reacted much differently, "Why wasn't I told of this before?" Parents must hear of their primacy, whether it's scary or gratifying, and we must be ready to give them a rationale behind our words asserting their importance to their children's ultimate faith life.

Dr. David Thomas, theologian and family life specialist, asserts that the basis for family theology is the foundational judgment that you are good and worthy of God's love. He calls the theological paradigm—*parents accept the child as God accepts us with all our faults and weaknesses*—"the most complex theological concept there is. Some people even accept it as mystery." He holds that real life creates good theology and, on the back-fence level, results in you-are-church ministry.

Rosemary Haughton, mother and theologian, stressed essentially the same idea in her paper at the Call to Action Hearing on Family:

> There is a passage which I think is not sufficiently recognized in the document on the laity which came out of the Second Vatican Council. The passage sketches in, almost in passing, it seems, a social role for the Christian family which is so extremely demanding that one has to read it several times to realize just what is being asked. It begins in a traditional fashion by calling on married couples to guard the sacredness of the marriage bond, but not only for themselves. . . . In this time of upheaval when so many innocent people are being hurt, there is an almost prophetic quality about that passage from the Council's document which firmly, almost ruthlessly, sets the Christian family at the heart of the church's mission of compassion for the world which God loves so much.
>
>   That, then, is the vocation of the family in the church —to discover its identity, to fulfill its needs, to grow in unity and loyalty by responding, each in its own way—to the Christian vocation of loving service. In each age, the church has called on special kinds of people to carry out its work. There is always a need for the religious congregation and other dedicated single people who can devote their lives to work beyond the scope and skill of an ordinary family. But it does seem that the church has a need at this particular historical moment for what a family can best provide: the sense of intimacy, the personal touch, a human environment of ordinary warmth and friendliness and lovingness.[9]

Also commenting on the role of the family in the *Decree on the Apostolate of the Laity,* Ferdinand Klostermann wrote:

> It is only because of the faith of its own family that a child can be baptized at all. The child's faith is an offshoot of the faith of the parents, and it is their faith which is to nourish the newborn faith until it grows and reaches maturity. If the family does not fulfill this charge, either because faith is lacking or because of indolence and laxity, then the faith of the child will normally fail to mature into a truly personal faith and will remain instead in an infantile state only to be rejected later or gradually to disappear. Sociological studies of the family show, in fact, how true this is. The religious

attitude and practice of young people is influenced by the family far beyond their early school years, far more than by companions or even one's work-milieu.[10]

Sociological data backs Klostermann's words. In their study of the impact of United States Catholic schools on American Catholics, Greeley and Rossi found that the religiousness of adult behavior was strongest when upbringing was in a family where the faith atmosphere was alive. "If our data from the past are any indication of the present situation, Catholic education is virtually wasted on three-fourths of those in Catholic schools because of the absence of a sufficiently religious family milieu."[11]

Andrew Greeley states emphatically that

> An analysis of the parochial school data by my colleague William McCready leaves no doubt at all that the most important predictor of religious performance of children is the religious behavior of their parents (and particularly their fathers) and the quality of the relationship between their mothers and fathers. . . .
>
> The elaborate statistical models he has developed leave no doubt at all that the parent is not only the principal educator but so important as an educator that all other educational institutions might almost be considered marginal in comparison. . . .
>
> In religious education the question is not family versus school (much less CCD versus school); the question is simply family with the school playing a modestly important but certainly secondary role of institutional socialization. "Phasing out" the schools isn't the answer. The critical question is, "How can we facilitate the work of the family?"[12]

In basically the same kind of study by Potvin, Hoge, and Nelson for the Boys Town Center for the Study of Youth Development and The Catholic University of America, the authors concluded:

> It is obvious from the data of Table 9 that the most important predictors of religiosity as measured by these indices are parental religious practice and whether or not the adolescent is currently studying religion. . . . Nonetheless there appears to be no substitute for a religious home environment and for religious instruction if adolescents are to remain committed to their religious heritage.[13]

Michael Novak, in a strong article on the family in *Harper's Magazine*, capsules all of these studies: "The family is a stronger agency of educational success than the school. The family is a stronger teacher of religious imagination than the church. . . . If things go well with the family, life is worth living; when the family falters, life falls apart."

The Second Vatican Council and recent episcopal statements abound concerning the primacy of the family in faith modeling and catechesis, but perhaps the recently published *National Catechetical Directory* reemphasizes it most strongly:

> Throughout the world the home is the crucial factor in determining children's overall performance. Behavioral disorders and social pathology in children and youth frequently begin in family disorganization: arising not only from within the family itself, but from the circumstances in which the family finds itself and from the way of life which results.
>
> Family and community are also extremely important in the catechetical process. While other factors are involved (e.g., age, sex, size of community, present study of religion, parental approval of the friends of their children, etc.), the impact of parents is primary among the human factors which influence this process. This is the principal reason for the current emphasis on preparation for parenthood and parent education, as well as a subsidiary motive for adult education.[14]

The statements and data exist, then, for a theology and a rationale for family catechesis, but they have not been generally accepted in the pew or in the family. Suggestions for helping parents, principals, and pastors to more readily envision and then perhaps accept the centrality of family catechesis will be offered later in this paper.

3 Sociology of the Family and of the Catholic Family

THE CHANGING FAMILY

Such immense sociological changes have impacted the family that I am reluctant to reduce them to mere statistics on divorce, the working mother, the influence of media, and other cultural pressures. Because diocesan directors seem so aware of the present sociology, I will focus on the old and new Catholic family in these pages. However, I wish to recommend a thorough treatment of the status of family in our society found in the work of The Carnegie Council on Children, *All Our Children: The American Family Under Pressure.*[15] The first section of the Carnegie book, "The Transformation of the Family," is particularly valuable in exposing old myths of the self-sufficient family and in describing changing functions of the American family today.

A second excellent source, recommended to me by family specialist Mary Novak of the Archdiocese of St. Paul and Minneapolis, is the tapes of lectures delivered by Dr. Richard Fowler of the Judson Family Institute in St. Paul.[16]

In these tapes, Dr. Fowler sketches the historical functions of the family: (1) economic; (2) protective; (3) religious; (4) status conferring; and (5) educational. He explains that gradually each of these functions shifted from the family to society. In the economic sphere, families shifted from productive to consumptive societies, and children from economic assets to liabilities. The protective function has been transferred to welfare and law enforcement agencies, the religious function to the Church, status conferring to job prestige and income, and education to the school system.

According to Fowler, when these historical functions began to disappear, there were dire predictions of the disappearance of the family (Hoover-Ogburn Report, 1934). But instead the family shifted functions, its primary ones now being the socialization of the children and the interpersonal relationships of its members. This shift in function brought with it powerful changes in value structures within the family, with egalitarian and companionate values predominating. Old value systems—where the father was the authoritarian earner, the mother the tender nurturer, and the children economic assets—are not helpful to today's family, although many leaders and spouses alike are intent on returning to "the way things should be." Parenting is confusing, because growing children tend to accept the new value system while parents are still struggling with the old.

To better understand the conflict between today's youth and their parents, we need to realize that there's more than just a traditional youth/adult rebellion occurring. Fowler asserts that while earlier generations rebelled *agewise,* today's youth is rebelling *valuewise,* and that creates an entirely new challenge to families. I heartily recommend this tape series to those involved in family ministry and catechesis.

THE CHANGING CATHOLIC FAMILY

The Catholic family has experienced even more change in function and identity in the past couple of decades. It has experienced the cultural shifts of the American family plus the shift from a strong church-centered family life to a more fragmented secular life. Many dioceses and catechists attempt to serve the family by anticipating the years to come and their impact on the family without looking back to the Catholic family of twenty-five or thirty years ago. Just as the family in society gradually changed its function, so the Catholic family gradually changed its relationship with the Church. Those very elements that once made the Catholic family unique are in flux. Its values are no longer as identifiably Catholic as they are American. Only after we are able to accept the present family and minister to it should we consider ministering to the family of the future.

Let's examine that family of the past. Twenty-five years ago, we all knew what the good Catholic family was like. We didn't have to define it. Many of us came from it. Today, we no longer use the adjective *good* partly because it is judgmental and partly, I suspect, because we aren't at all sure we ourselves would be included in our own definition. Here is my profile.

Yesterday's Good Catholic Family

- It had two parents.
- Both parents were Catholic.
- There were many children.
- Mom was at home.
- This was a parish-centered family deriving its educational, welfare, social, and spiritual life from the parish.
- There was weekly family attendance at confession and Mass.
- There was faithful attendance at parish school or CCD religious instruction.
- There was much parent-child contact.
- Parents had strict control over influences on children.
- There was a slower pace of life.
- The family was supportive of the pastor and parish staff regardless of their ideology.
- The ultimate judgment of this family was the religious outcome of the children. If they grew up to marry Catholics and remain supportive and active parishioners, the parents were considered successful parents.

Today's Catholic Family

- It might have two parents. According to *The National Catechetical Directory,* currently about one family in every five with school-aged children is headed by one parent. According to Dr. Richard Fowler, 40 percent of the children of marriages of the 70s will some time live in a single parent home. We have no way of assessing accurately how many Catholic families are headed by one parent because many families join the ranks of the unchurched when they are divorced, but we do know that the Catholic divorce rate grows closer to the national divorce rate yearly.
- In slightly more than half of today's Catholic families, both parents are Catholic. Statistics vary, but according to William McCready, "only 67 percent of the Catholics are in marriages where both partners are Catholic. There is no trend data available on this point, but many observers have reported that mixed marriages among Catholics and Protestants have been growing."[17] This statistic led Jerry Sexton of National Marriage Encounter to point out that "we are on the cutting edge of ecumenism." It may also

18

explain increasing interest in ecumenism among grass-roots Catholics. In a study done for the Catholic Press Association by Gallup in 1977, 84 percent of those surveyed said that the Church should become more ecumenical.[18] This was the highest percentage responding positively to a large number of issues offered.[18]

- There are fewer children. The Catholic birth rate runs almost parallel with the national birth rate.
- Mom will work outside the home sometime during the child-rearing years. Seventy-five percent of today's mothers of children between the ages of six and seventeen work outside the home at least part time. Even more impressive is the finding of the 1975 White House Commission on Women that only 9 percent of the women surveyed under age thirty said they planned to be just housewives and mothers during their lifetime. A 1977 study by the Bureau of Labor Statistics shows that only 22 percent of tax-paying family units are the "typical" family of working father, homemaker mother, and one, two, or more children. The other 78 percent of family units are made up of two working parents or the single parent or couples without children.
- The parish is not the center of family life today. The Catholic family is into society both economically and socially today. French theologian Jacques Piveteau drew a visual analogy to show the change. He said that yesterday's child was surrounded by a series of concentric circles beginning with the individual, then family, then Church, then community, while today's family is represented by intersecting circles like puzzle pieces. Families find that analogy apt as does psychologist Kenneth Keniston who claims ". . . parents today have a demanding new role choosing, meeting, talking with, and coordinating the experts, the technology, and the institutions that help bring up their children. The specific work involved is familar to any parent: consultations with teachers, finding good health care, trying to monitor television watching, and so on."[19]
- Sunday Mass, confession, and religion class are not as important as they once were. Fewer than fifty percent of today's Catholics attend Mass weekly, with confession attendance even less. In 1976, according to "An Update of

'Where Are the 6.6 Million?'" (published by the United States Catholic Conference), an estimated 7.7 million Catholic youngsters were receiving no formal religious instruction.

- Fewer than one-fourth of the nation's Catholics are enrolled in Catholic schools. This varies from area to area with the heaviest attendance on the East Coast and in large metropolitan areas.
- There is an ever-decreasing amount of parent-child contact. Divorce, working mothers, absentee fatherhood because of job demands, television, and increased activity schedules on the part of children severely cut into parent-child time together. One study in which 300 eighth-grade boys were asked to keep a log of the amount of time spent alone with their fathers in a two-week period disclosed that the average boy spent fifteen minutes alone with his father in a two-week period.
- Parents have little control over influences on children today. Although parents remain the primary influence, peer influence takes over at age twelve, and television remains the second most pervasive child-shaper today.
- Families are experiencing a rapid, even frenetic, pace of life. In the average family, the calendar determines communication time, prayer time, and socialization. Religious educators trying to involve parents in more family-togetherness activity frequently hear, "We can't get together to eat, much less to pray." Part-time jobs, school activities, sports, meetings, lessons all infringe upon family time. Even children say, "Is it Christmas already?" The family inherits everyone else's calendar—school, church, organized sports, Scouts. Marshall McLuhan made a perceptive observation when he said that American families are public places from which they must escape into the public for privacy. Families often have to get out of town to be truly together. Couples have to go out to dinner to really converse and communicate.

When I wrote as my first column of 1977, "A Year to Slow Down," I was astonished at the reaction from readers. I listed eighty activities on which families spend time, excluding necessary functions like dental appointments, and I suggested that readers ask their families to prioritize the items in order of preference. The response was remarkably similar. Families themselves were surprised to discover they put a high priority on simple family-togetherness times like hiking, fixing the car together, camping, fishing, or just taking a walk. Conversely, they and their children liked least the highly organized activities that today's parents feel are necessary to the development of their children.

- Families are not automatically supportive of the pastor, staff, or parish ideology. They question decisions and often step over parish boundary lines if they find the liturgy, the educational structure, or the staff not to their liking.

- The ultimate judgment of today's Catholic parents is not whether their children marry Catholics and stay within the Church but if their children grow up with some values, see marriage as a worthy institution, and are motivated toward some kind of career goals. With chemical dependency, depression and suicide, and with non-marital relationships so prevalent and attractive to today's young people, parents simply have higher concerns than the Catholic marriage. Since this removes the visible factor of parental success from Catholic parenting, Catholic parents aren't sure what a good Catholic parent must do or be today. The function of Catholic parenting has changed, but the new function has not been defined.

What percentage of today's families in (and out of) the pew match each of the above profiles? We must not fall into the trap of presuming that our families are the stereotypic good Catholic families of yesterday and of writing programs to minister to them. If we do, we will be ministering to a fraction of our real families. Urie Bronfenbrenner remarked, "I only wish we could examine today's family without nostalgia. We could learn something about its great strengths and its terrible weaknesses and could see our task more clearly."

Nostalgia has been costly to our Church. Much effort has been expended in finding someone to blame for the new family and in attempting to get back to yesterday's family. It isn't a very productive effort. We have focused on scapegoating too long. For some time, we blamed Vatican Council II, but this blaming became ineffective when Protestant and Jewish families showed the same kinds of shifts. A colleague of mine in Jewish family education once said wistfully, "I wish we had a Council to blame."

The *Pro Mundi Vita* paper on the Western family stated it baldly:

> We start with the fact that the social changes which have affected the family so radically have upset traditional pastoral care so much as to cause the Church to lose an increasing amount of the outstanding social control which for a long time was hers in this domain.[20]

Whose fault it is, this new family, isn't important. Certain societal changes have wrought a different family model from any other in history, and this family has different needs. How we identify and address these needs is foundational to our eventual results in family catechetical efforts.

4 Needs in the Catholic Family of Today

ASSESSING THE NEEDS

This section is an assessment of needs as derived from our most recent reports—the 1976 Call to Action Consultation and *The Report on the Twelve Regional Meetings of Diocesan Family Directors* (1977). In studying the reports, I realized that while the enumerated needs are often the same, actions to meet those needs are articulated from different perspectives, i.e., the perspective of the family in the Call to Action Consultation and the perspective of the helping professionals in the Church (Family Life Directors). While this doesn't minimize the needs and problems themselves, a combined listing might distort proposed actions.

An example: The Call to Action respondents, primarily parents, clearly asked for help in achieving better marriages through professional marriage counseling, communication skills, and healthier sexuality education. They rarely mentioned the need for a theology of marriage or an understanding of permanent commitment—two needs which appeared frequently on the Family Life Directors' (primarily clergy) report. The needs are understandably linked, but listing them together might give an erroneous impression as to their validity.

Because I served as a writer on the Family Committee of the Call to Action Consultation and worked on the feedback from parents from the beginning, I will take the liberty of sharing some personal observations. First, the high number of issues/actions under the umbrella of *family* surprised groundwork committees who originally supposed other areas of social action interest would surpass *family*. For some months, *family* led significantly in the number of issues submitted from around the country, ultimately ending up second to Church. Perhaps respondents were telling us that until their needs in the most intimate community are met, they cannot get deeply interested in ministering to others.

Secondly, the same issues or needs rose to the top and stayed there. Our first computer printout reached us in

March, 1976 and numbered about 30,000 issues/actions. Ultimately, the consultation numbered over 800,000 responses, but the same top issues held. They changed positions in various printouts but they held steadily regardless of diocese of origin. Interestingly, responses from laity in the so-called "conservative" and "liberal" dioceses were remarkably similar. From this, we may presume that family needs across the country are similar, and that diocesan leadership's ideology doesn't unduly influence these needs.

Thirdly, while there has been much debate over the representation of the delegates in Detroit, it's important to remember that the Consultation exists of and by itself. If there had been no Detroit meeting, we would still have the Consultation as a need indicator, the first that we have ever had from large numbers of Catholics across dioceses.

CALL TO ACTION CONSULTATION—FAMILY

Specific needs and issues are categorized under general areas which I list in order from most to least frequent responses. Although these are based on 700,000 responses rather than the final 825,000, the order remained the same in the final printout.

1. Support of Family Values

- By far the most frequently mentioned area in which parents want help from their Church is reinforcement of the value of family. Families today feel lonely and alone in trying to rear good children. With increasing numbers of couples choosing to have children later or to have fewer or no children, couples committed to family values find themselves unsure and defensive with little institutional support.
- Parents need help in teaching values, respect, dignity, and a healthy self-image in themselves and in their children.
- Parents requested more family prayer and worship activities like the home Mass. Interestingly, families did not indicate that old forms of family devotion such as the rosary, novenas, and the like were useful in today's family, but they asked for a return to the religious traditions that gave a spiritual dimension to their own childhood lives. The closest they came to describing this was "worship

activities like the home Mass." It seems clear that families are asking for new spiritual forms and traditions which will appeal to today's family. This is a challenge to all involved in family catechesis.

- Parents asked for help in re-instilling cultural traditions in the family. This was particularly important to Hispanic Catholics who number nearly one-fourth of our country's Catholics.

2. Family-Life Education Programs

- Parents requested parish and diocesan programs in parenting skills of all types. Specific programs such as Parent Effectiveness Training and Dreikurs were mentioned as examples, but plea after plea was made by parents to "help us to be better parents." Several respondents made the point that pre-baptismal preparation was a start, but it was involved more in making them good Catholic parents than in making them good parents.

- Realistic premarital, marital, and divorce preparation was also called for. Marriage Encounter was mentioned, but so was a frequent request for marriage enrichment for those turned off by the encounter-type weekend, for those in mixed marriages, and for those who are seeking a ministry together which reaches beyond their marriage.

- Sexuality education for both children and parents was requested. Parents are clearly unhappy with the Church's lack of assistance in helping them foster practical, solid, and moral education in sexuality for themselves and their children. Almost any good sexuality program would be welcomed by parents.

- Parents are searching for help in dealing with the aged, handicapped, and other family members who need special or extraordinary care.

3. Divorced

- Respondents requested a change in attitude toward the divorced in our Church. It was pointed out in numerous hearings that the attitude goes deeper than just Church law, that the people in the pew often make the divorced and families of the divorced seem unwelcome. As Father James Young, Paulist mentor of the largest organization for divorced and separated Catholics in America, said in a speech to Family Life Directors in Denver in 1977, "Catholics who have undergone the pain of divorce often must undergo the pain of losing favor in their Church, also. Just when they need support the most, it is withdrawn." Response bears out his words.

- Respondents requested that parishes and dioceses focus on both social and spiritual needs of the divorced. The divorced feel that everything is designed for couples and families, yet they have unique spiritual and social needs. Few parishes have special functions or groups for the divorced in their midst.

4. Communication Skills

- Parents requested that the Church teach families how to communicate with one another, their Church, and their school. Again, Parent Effectiveness Training, Marriage Encounter, and the parent communication program DEKA I and II were mentioned as models deserving of imitation.

    (When I listed these top eight issues in my weekly column and asked readers to rate them, they placed communication as the top rather than the fourth need. It would seem that communication within the family should receive top priority in parish family programming.)

5. Pressures against Family Life

- Respondents asked for help in offsetting the values promoted by television and movies which are contrary to Christian life. (The negative influence of television pervaded the entire Call to Action Consultation. The response concerning the media was difficult to categorize. Interestingly, the media was mentioned as an issue or problem. However, respondents seldom suggested action for overcoming the problem. Parents are apparently frustrated at the impact of the mass media, but they don't know what to do about it. It's fair to say that it looms as a major problem in families.)
- They also sought assistance in handling the new permissiveness, drugs, alcohol, advertising, mobility, music, affluence, unemployment, and the changing attitudes of women.
- They requested help in controling family activities and returning to a quieter pace of life.

6. Counseling

- Respondents requested professional marriage, family, and particularly parent/teen counseling from their Church.

7. Family Sense of Vocation/Social Witness

An excellent reference to these needs can be found in Dr. Rosemary Haughton's paper delivered at the Call to Action hearing on *family* in Atlanta and printed in *Origins,* August 28, 1975 (NC Documentary Service, USCC, Washington, DC).

- Respondents asked for help in developing a sense of compassion in the family living in today's consumer-oriented culture.
- They specifically requested help in learning how to be ministering families reaching out to others.
- They asked for vehicles and structures in the parish for viable family-to-family ministry.

8. Single Parenting

- Widowed and divorced Catholic parents feel as if they are getting little support as parents from their church. They requested activities in which the missing-parent role models would be present and shared; they asked for efforts toward making single parents more welcome in the parish, and for help in parenting alone, in spirituality, and in dealing with loneliness.

FAMILY LIFE DIRECTORS' REPORT

The Family Life Directors' Report was compiled by the twelve regional directors representing family life personnel from the 186 dioceses. The twelve regions reported a total of 155 articulated needs. I tabulated the top 104 in order below. The number at left represents the number of times an issue was mentioned. (The first item was mentioned twice in one regional report.) Readers should understand that each mention of a need represents at least fifteen dioceses.

| 13 | *Divorce* | The conglomerate of problems dealing with troubled marriages, the separated and divorced, and the civilly remarried |

9	*Women's Movement*	The changing attitude of women in our culture and the change in male and female roles in the traditional family makeup
9	*Theology*	Lack of a real theology of marriage, family, and sexuality
8	*Values*	Lack of goals and values for being Christian, uncertainty about the meaning of Christianity as it applies to the family
7	*Permanency*	Lack of a sense of permanent commitment in marriage
7	*Leadership*	Need for a more sensitive awareness by clergy and Church personnel in dealing with couples and families
7	*Confusion*	Great confusion over the significance and purpose of marriage today, especially over the procreative meaning of marriage
7	*Identity*	Lack of faith formation for a Catholic identity
7	*Family Ministry*	Lack of priority given family-life programs and support systems in dioceses and parishes
6	*Sexuality*	Need for promotion and development of sexuality education and family-living education at all levels
5	*Isolation*	Isolation of the family from the community of other families, loss of the extended family
5	*Family as Minister*	Need to design and develop self-help ministry for couples and families
5	*Media*	The media, especially television, undermine responsible ideals of marriage and family life
4	*Clergy*	Need for ongoing clergy education, especially in the area of family ministry
4	*Parenting*	Need to re-educate parents to understand and handle their role as parents
3	*Support*	Lack of positive support in our Church and culture for family ideals

It is interesting to study the two reports together because one is compiled from the perspective of parents, "What we need," and one from Church personnel, "What *they* (families) need." While the two are divergent in places, there is a strong similarity in pinpointing areas of need in today's family.

Note the significant difference in the placement of the changing attitude and role of women. In the Call to Action Consultation, this placed fifth and was listed along with pressures against family life. The Family Life Directors, placing it second (with nine regions representing 135 dioceses), viewed it as a far stronger influence in the lived experience of the modern family. Why the discrepancy? Possibly because the variety of women's issues landed in several areas in the Call to Action Consultation—*Church, Personhood,* and *Work*—so that when it was tallied under *Family,* it was only a woman's role as it pertained to her family. A more likely reason is that the Family Life Directors, as helping professionals, recognize the impact of the changing attitudes of women on the family more clearly than do the husbands and wives themselves. There is a need for more accurate data on this.

It appears as if "Support for Family Values" topped one list and bottomed the other, but it is a rather ambiguously stated need. I believe one reason it received so many issues in the Call to Action Consultation is that it absorbed the religion-in-the-home actions. Conspicuously absent from both lists is religious education. Perhaps we are gaining a broader sense of religion. Perhaps families feel it is less significant alongside greater needs, i.e., learning doctrine doesn't seem so vital if the adolescent hasn't spoken to anyone for three weeks, as the mother indicated in one of the opening quotes in this paper. Or respondents feel that the Church is already emphasizing religious education so there wasn't a need to mention it. (While parish schools and religious education appeared under the category of *Church* in the Consultation, it had more to do with formal programs than family-centered faith.)

Finally, I think we should consider what kind of Catholic was most likely to respond to the Call to Action Consultation. We have no data, but when the Indiana

Catholic Conference consulted its laity in 1975, it discovered that the average respondent was white, female, and over thirty-five years old. This tends to be the kind of Catholic who attends meetings, completes survey forms, and takes part in parish discussion groups—the general work force in most parishes. If the Call to Action Consultation respondents mirror Indiana, we are operating on information from less than half the churched and on no information from the unchurched, who now number nearly half our Catholics. Missing is vital information from younger couples, families, minorities, and lay males.

5 Meeting Expressed Needs in the Diocese and in the Parish

DEVELOPING A PLAN FOR FAMILY MINISTRY

As a result of the numerous and urgent requests made of the Church by its members, the American bishops authorized an Ad Hoc Commission on Marriage and Family to draw up a plan to address these needs holistically. The resulting Plan of Pastoral Action for Family Ministry was passed by the bishops unanimously in May of 1978. It would be ideal but unwieldy to publish the Plan here. Significant to our purposes are strategies, timetables, and coordination.

The Plan is a process based first on listening to the family in individual dioceses and parishes. Needs like those listed in the previous section are national indicators of need, but they may vary widely from parish to parish. A pastoral listening and planning workbook, *Sounds of the Family,* instructs diocesan teams on how to listen and how to meet the needs in the parish and diocese. Calling family ministry "the Church's newest vineyard," the Plan targets six areas of ministry:

> One: Ministry to Pre-Marrieds and Singles
> Two: Ministry for Married Couples
> Three: Ministry for Parents
> Four: Ministry for "Developing" Families
> Five: Ministry for "Hurting" Families
> Six: Ministry for Leadership Couples and Families

The authors tell us,

> Certainly these areas of ministry will touch several diocesan offices as well as families and lay workers in different ministries. . . . "Developing" families include those that need spirituality, sacramental preparation, home prayer programs, family "nights" and "days," and parish family liturgies. This could involve the interests of the religious education, schools, and liturgy offices.
> "Hurting" families include those struggling with poverty, aging, alcoholism, drug abuse, homosexuality, and separated, divorced, and handicapped members. This could include the

activities touched on by the Catholic Charities, Tribunal and youth offices, as well as the family life office or bureau.

Ministry for leadership couples and families includes parish coordinating couples, family social-action couples, and leaders in family movements. This could involve the adult education, social justice and pastoral commission offices, and the family life commission members.[21]

The Plan itself spells out specific timetables and leadership responsibilities pertinent to our work in family catechesis.

It (diocesan planning) is to be coordinated by the diocesan family-life committee or advisory board working in cooperation with other diocesan agencies, such as education and Catholic Charities offices. The diocesan family life office is to take the initiative in this process through its director who should oversee the planning process as well as other family-related programs, organizations, and movements.[22]

It is evident that coordination between offices is pivotal to meeting the family catechetical challenge of the 1980s. If diocesan directors continue to view sacramental preparation, home spirituality, and parenting education as theirs without coordination and cooperation, while family life offices and diocesan family teams view the responsibility as theirs, great duplication, confusion, and even dissention might result. This does not have to occur, but it is a hazard better mentioned in these early stages than experienced later.

In light of the requests by diocesan directors of this author to address the very areas being addressed by the Plan, it seems essential that education offices begin by seeking coordination, offering assistance, and sharing the ministry in order to develop a holistic approach to family catechesis.

Father Donald Conroy, representative for Family Life at the USCC and chief architect of the Plan, foresaw the need for coordination back in 1975 in a speech to family life directors gathered for their annual convention in New Orleans:

We need to open and keep open the channels of communication with other commissions and offices diocesanwide and nationally. We should be aware that there are many activities of mutual interest to other diocesan apostolates and agencies. Most often, family life is seen from an educational or charities perspective. Consequently, we need to have good communications with these offices and, if we are under either "umbrella," as I am under education at the United States Catholic Conference, we need to explain and defend family life ministry as a valid and viable pastoral activity of immense practical importance.[23]

A CATECHESIS FOR MEETING
EXPRESSED NEEDS IN THE PARISH

Because a great number of diocesan directors requested information on family catechetical programs, both those that have been successful and those that have failed, I will focus specifically on those in this section. In 1976, I was asked to deliver at a major religious education congress an analysis of operating and defunct family programs. In my research, I found that there are certain key factors or indicators of success operating in parishes with effective family programs. They follow in order of importance.

1. Shared pastoral vision on the importance of family-centered catechesis is the most significant predictor of parish success. If the pastor and religious education staff are convinced that family-centered catechesis is central and that all other religious instruction—school, CCD, and adult education—is peripheral to family, parishioners tend to respond. They sense action emanating from a philosophy. If only one staff member, however, is convinced of the primacy and value, the program isn't nearly so effective. My mail attests to the number of pastors who give verbal encouragement but withdraw it at the first sign of criticism or difficulty. On the other hand, many pastors who are solidly committed to the primacy of family education are unsuccessful in transmitting this vision to coordinators and volunteer teachers who, nevertheless, try to carry out the pastor's philosophy. The results are often mixed and disappointing.

Maureen Gallagher, whom I interviewed for this paper, emphasized this factor. When asked to explain parishes where *Family* was effective for awhile and then lost its attraction, she said, "It's almost always due to a shift in personnel. Either a new pastor comes in with an instructional model of religious education, or the original DRE leaves and is replaced by one who doesn't share the vision of family-centered catechesis."

This leads into the matter of trust between staff and people. Clarice Flagel of St. Pius X Parish in Cedar Rapids, Iowa, and DRE in a parish that has had a viable family program for a number of years, puts trust between catechists and families at the top of the list. "If there's trust, there are volunteers. If there's trust, there's commitment, and if there's commitment, faith is usually present," she asserts. She credits tenure of staff as a factor in building that trust in a parish that easily involves 150 volunteers annually in the family-to-family programs offered.

Experiences in parishes where family programs have failed point out that tenure of the pastor and the DRE play an important part in developing trust. In parishes where there is a new coordinator every two years, people are less trusting of new ideas and less willing to commit themselves to support something as radical as a change from classroom model to family model of religious instruction.

Parish motivation, then, should be a basic question. Why a family-centered program? Because the bishop says so? Because nothing else is working? Because the parish next door has one? Or because the staff is truly convinced that it is the ideal in fostering a strong faith life? Only the last reason is good enough.

2. Parish preparation or pre-evangelization is a second key factor. Often there is no preparation at all. Parishioners aren't educated to the need but are informed of the change. In the family programs that fail, lack of preparation of parents looms as a major cause. When people are asked to change a total system of education—from classroom to home, from nun to family, from basics to faith—they have years of conditioning to overcome. A catchy slogan and parish pep talk simply aren't enough. Parishes with the most successful family programs are those that take the longest time to prepare parishioners for change. Some even set aside formal instruction for a year to focus on parent preparation.

At this time, parents must be given some indication of projected educational timetables in the parish. In the past, many parents accepted that their young children were too immature to learn doctrine only to discover that when the children were mature enough to understand it, there was no doctrinal instruction available to them in the parish. These parents witnessed their own youth leaving home with little or no understanding of their faith or Church. Their experience planted seeds of distrust in parents of younger children. The pre-evangelization period can include sessions and homilies on cognitive learning, data on the importance of parents to the religious socialization of the child, and timetables showing emphasis on family education when children are young and on formal classroom and peer education when children are capable of conceptualizing.

One parish staff utilized the first three months of a year's suspension of formal classes for children to study the parish and published models of family programs. They then drew up this sketchy "scope and sequence" together and used it successfully to explain the program to parishioners and get their enthusiastic cooperation:

Parish-Family Education—Scope and Sequence

Pre- and post-baptismal parenting
- Giving parents a vision of themselves as primary faith enrichers and an enthusiasm for initiating a strong faith environment in the family.
- Affirming young parents in their role
- Teaching parents some basic parenting techniques
- Giving parents an understanding of cognitive and moral development
- Facilitating support groups from which natural leaders emerge

School-age parenting
- Developing awareness of needs of personhood, whether single, married, or divorced
- Creating a rich and ongoing faith environment in the family—prayer, rituals, celebration
- Parenting courses
- Sacramental preparation
- Ongoing ministry to others in the parish family

- Healthy liturgical experiences
- Dealing with TV, friends, school

Pre-adolescent parenting
- Need for peer education among eleven- and twelve-year olds
- Beginning of formal religious instruction
- Social interaction, value setting
- Parent education on changing adolescents

Adolescent parenting
- Parent-teen communication techniques
- Family pressures—chemical dependency, sexuality, mobility
- Value setting
- Scripture and formal religious instruction by professional teachers available to parish teens
- Confirmation (optional at this time)

Post-parenting
- Dealing with changing roles and identity
- Empty-nest syndrome
- Utilizing skills and time to aid and affirm others
- Developing second careers
- Ongoing adult education
- Offering spiritual, educational, and social programs for singles, widowed, and/or elderly

The above goals were not intended to be complete, but they were used to show parishioners how lifelong faith nourishment can be a realistic parish goal and to convince them that the staff was implementing a well-planned program rather than a fad. The staff was convinced that their clarity of purpose and indication of a well thought-out plan for the parish, not for just a year or two, but for family life spans, contributed to acceptance and success in an originally suspicious parish.

3. *The ability of the staff to develop or adapt a published program to fit the needs of the people is a significant factor of success.* The first emphasis must be on people, not on programs. I doubt if any program will meet the needs of a rural community, a middle-class suburban parish, an inner-city parish, an Hispanic parish, an industrial-area parish, and a military

base. There shouldn't be such a program. Parishes that have studied their people, asked them what they need and want, and designed or adapted a published program suitable to the lifestyle and education level of parishioners are having the greatest success.

Most of the authors of published programs call for this adaptation to suit the parish, but I recall the situation in a midwest parish where a coordinator transferred from the diocesan office to a small rural community so she could test her assumptions in family-centered catechesis. She bought complicated programs and used numerous sophisticated value and communication techniques. This was a highly settled area where children were content to stay on the farm and more or less accept their parents' values, and they couldn't relate to her leadership. She was unsuccessful because the parishioners didn't relate to *her* needs.

4. True family-centered efforts, as opposed to child-centered, through the family have proved more effective. As many directors wisely noted on their survey sheets, true family-centered catechetics should not be seen as just another way of getting a message to the children. Yet, many parish goals seem to be just that. The family is seen as an alternate channel for conveying religious instruction rather than as a faith community which needs to develop its own faith environment. Unfortunately, our emphasis on sacramental preparation, while certainly a valuable prelude to family-centered catechesis, can give parents the impression that the family becomes the teacher responsible for instructing the children in fundamentals pertaining to the sacrament. Parishes with a keen vision of family catechesis are more interested in the faith climate at home than evidence of it at Church. According to Sandra DeGidio, OSM, "It is important to remember always that the family-program structure that takes place at the parish is only a stimulus and impetus for what actually takes place within and outside the family. Family catechesis bears fruit away from us, not in front of us."[24]

5. The quality of liturgical participation in the parish is another indicator of success. Once families experience faith community, whether they are couples who have made a Marriage Encounter, singles who become involved in social action, or families who have learned to communicate together, they expect and anticipate a community liturgy that is alive and caring. If the liturgies in the parish are dull, repetitious, and non-participatory, families are apt to seek liturgical expression outside the parish, and the parish as family-of-families will suffer. We find the most successful family programs in parishes with the most liturgical participation.

6. *Allocation of resources in the parish is another factor.* Some parishes taking on family-centered catechesis presume there's little need for a budget. The thinking goes that since learning doesn't require classrooms and teachers, there will be few costs. Good family catechesis calls for qualified parish personnel to help families—counselors, workshop leaders of all kinds, communication specialists—as well as resources for retreats, liturgical celebrations, offices, telephones, and extraneous expenses. Where family programs are left to dedicated but untrained volunteers without budgets, all the good will in the world won't insure effectiveness.

7. *The existence of some type of formal instruction for children concomitant with family-centered catechesis is another factor of success.* Many parents who agree to become part of family-centered programs do so out of doubt. They don't *really* believe that they are their children's most important religious educators. They were taught too well that only Father or Sister could really teach children religion, and they are reluctant to abandon that comfort simply because the parish espouses family faith. Until they experience the depth of faith possible in family-centered catechesis, it is wise to continue to offer some kind of class or occasional workshop for the children, not for the sake of the children, but to free the parents from the concern that their children might not "learn" enough from them. This freedom from concern empowers parents to focus on their own faith life. The most successful parishes give a nod, at least, to formal peer education. Some give one half-day a month, others offer a week or

two of summer school. Many parishes mistakenly presume that if they close down all formal religious instruction for children, parents will be attracted to family-centered programs. In reality, these parents feel driven to it, which they often resent, and they spend their energies trying to reinstate classes for their children. By offering both—family catechesis in ever increasing amounts and formal instruction for children in ever decreasing amounts—many parishes are finding success.

Other indicators of success include parishes whose intention it is to serve the family rather than mold it; parishes who offer choices in scheduling for active families; parishes who view youth as an integral part of family; parishes who utilize family-to-family ministry; parishes with strong social action programs; and parishes who constantly affirm and support their families. The reverse of these are parishes whose hidden agenda is to get back to the good Catholic family of the past; parishes who offer each course, lecture, or ritual once and, if the family can't make it, the parish is absolved of responsibility; parishes who totally separate youth, singles, and retired from family programs; and parishes who use fear rather than affirmation to motivate families.

6 Models of Family Programs

According to Sandra DeGidio, OSM, who has written what I consider the best available work on family-centered catechetical programs, *Sharing Faith in the Family: A Guide to Ritual and Catechesis* (Twenty-Third Publications, West Mystic, CT, 1980), there are five basic models of family programs presently being used around the country. With her permission, I am listing the five here with a condensed version of her description and the advantages and disadvantages of each.

PEER-GROUP CENTERED   This is the popular format introduced by the Paulist *Family* program in which children and their parents are brought together from one to three times a month, separated into learning groups, and gathered for an activity and Eucharist or closing prayer. Many parishes hold the program on Sunday morning, others during the week.

Advantages: It's a good transitional model from the usual parish CCD program to the addition of classes for parents at the same time. The fact that children and parents are concentrating on the same subject enables them to continue discussion and ritual at home. By holding classes at the same time and by requiring only one or two trips monthly for religious education of the whole family, this program doesn't fragment the family as some others do. Adult education is an integral part of this model, i.e., if the children are to attend, their parents must attend.

Disadvantages: According to Sister Sandra, ". . . it is not really a family model but an extended CCD model which is making some of the same mistakes that we are already making: namely that religion is something to be learned." There isn't much time for generational sharing. The value of this model is its transitional use. Once a parish is comfortable with the idea of total family education, it can leave this model and innovate according to its perceived needs.

FAMILY LEARNING TEAMS   Joseph and Mercedes Iannone are best known in the Catholic Church for piloting and promoting this model which is designed around the open classroom learning-center concept. Neighborhood groups of fifteen or so families take on the religious education responsibility for one another in their geographical area. Each adult is expected to contribute in some way—teaching children, planning liturgies, providing hospitality, and the like.

Advantages: It is great for community building and for fostering the small-parish concept found in many dioceses throughout the country. This model is able to involve singles and seniors and provides a good deal of adult education through training those who teach the children. Finally, it can meet a plurality of needs because each group is encouraged to be autonomous rather than interdependent. This is a good model to initiate if people in the parish want to get to know one another on a more intimate basis.

Disadvantages: Once again, the emphasis is on learning, primarily on the education of children. "The Learning Center activities are often designed for children, the emphasis is again on learning, and parents tend to participate because it is good for their children, and out of a sense of responsibility to one another's children," writes Sister Sandra. Still, the structure is here for a wider area of ministry and can be easily adapted to areas like family communication, parenting courses, social ministry, and the like.

FAMILY CLUSTERS   Margaret Sawin is the well-known originator of this concept which is structured around groups of four or five families or twenty-five people who gather together for a six-week period of initial sessions on communication and then expand to study and discuss topics which are selected by the group. This is a family group in the broad sense of the term, explicitly including couples whose children have grown, singles, elderly, and families with children of all ages. Participants are required to sign a contract to stay with the group for the entire session, thus eliminating early dropouts which plague some of the other models.

Advantages: This model is good for grouping people of all ages with like interests and, if it is structured geographically, it can be a fine community builder. Several parishes have found it effective in helping parishioners to communicate with one another and their church. It is open-ended, so it doesn't suffer the juvenile-learning emphasis of other models. Like Family Learning Teams, it provides an extended-family structure for those seeking one.

Disadvantages: Clusters are not developmentally organized. Ideally, participants are expected to grow from one topic and session to another, but this is often not the case. Parents do not see it as a part of a long-range family growth and development process. In fact, many families sign up for one six-week session and then presume they have taken the course or met their adult education responsibility. Finally, there is need for a coordinator trained in the process, and this is not always feasible.

LITURGY MODEL   This model uses the Sunday liturgy for educational as well as liturgical purposes. Generally, participants are divided into groups of parents, teens, and children to discuss the homily and lessons it encompasses for thirty or forty-five minutes; they then come together to celebrate the Liturgy of the Eucharist and conclude with coffee and doughnuts.

According to Sister Sandra, its only advantage is that it is convenient for both families and parishes. She says, "Frankly, I do not see it as a valid model of family catechesis. It is a misuse of the liturgy as well as a misuse of catechetics. The liturgy is not a means or method of education; the liturgy is the time that the community gathers to worship. It is the community's opportunity to come together to remember and solemnize its lived experiences, to waste time with the Lord, to complete what is already in process, to, as John Shea says, tell the story and break the bread. It is not a time to be educated."

Her words echo my experience with parishes who have tried this model. It tends to divide, not unite the parish community, by setting aside one liturgy for families and the others for everyone else. If we're serious about the idea that everyone in the parish family is also a family, then we need communal worship. I know of no parish that has stayed with this model for long.

SACRAMENTAL HOPSCOTCHING   This is my term for the regrettable model of family catechesis found in many parishes which is not family catechesis at all but parental assistance in preparing the children for the sacraments. Rarely does it form the basis for an ongoing faith-enrichment effort in the family, rather, it ends with a particular child's reception of a sacrament. In many ways, this is counterproductive to family-centered catechesis because it indicates to parent and child alike that faith is consumed in gulps every few years when the church decides it is important for parent and child to sit together and do a number of projects in order to develop a relationship with God.

What goes on in the total family during this preparation or between preparations is often of little interest to the parish. I recall the couple who had a child involved in each of the three traditional preparations simultaneously—eucharist, penance, and confirmation—so for a couple of months they spent at least two evenings weekly at the parish church. The family was fragmented by the parish calendar, and everyone talked wistfully about "when we get through with the sacraments." There was also an envy on the part of three other non-involved children because the parents were spending so much time with their siblings. How much better it would have been if the preparation took place within the framework of an ongoing family faith-enrichment program that was a natural part of the family's daily life.

However, there is an advantage in involving parents in sacramental preparation if it's seen as a prelude to family catechesis. It can, as Sister Sandra indicates, serve as an initiation into further participation in family catechesis and also as a form of pre-evangelization for family programs in the parish. I have seen many parents become involved in parish through their children's sacramental preparation which also eventually lead them into an ongoing family faith program.

To Sister Sandra's five models, I would like to add two.

FAMILY NIGHT   Initially based on the Mormon format of setting aside one night weekly for the family without interruption from television, meetings, or other activities, this is becoming an increasingly popular response to the chaos experienced by many families. In this model, which is too new to evaluate (and probably never destined to appeal to a majority of parish parents), parents receive materials and instruction once a month or at the beginning of each Church season and undertake a family night weekly or bi-monthly. Usually, there is some scripture reading, meditation, game, discussion, and shared prayer. The possibilities are broad and bear watching in the few parishes that have experimented with this model. I know a coordinator with a highly successful family program based on a composite of the above models. She "heard" the frustration of her parents over the constant call to leave home in order to find God in each other through Church, and she offered them materials to try a weekly family night at home as an alternative. To her astonishment, twelve families took up her initial offer. The number doubled the second year, and she sees it as a viable direction in family catechesis. Controlling the family calendar is of high value in many families and a family-night model might be the answer for a parish with a high number of overly committed families.

FAMILY RETREAT Several dioceses and parishes are experimenting with a family retreat model of catechesis, and where it has been tried, results look good. However, because it simply isn't feasible to involve a great number of families in retreats, some parishes have opted for sponsoring mustard-seed and leadership families at retreats, expecting them to return to be an integral part of parish family efforts. Other parishes hold day retreats for the family, where the entire family attends on Friday evening, all day Saturday, and half of Sunday but returns home to sleep. Family retreats (sometimes called renewals) include family communication sessions, family prayer and rituals, family sexuality, the workings of God within the family, and the like. Early efforts in this direction seem promising.

By the time this book appears in print, there may well be other models of family catechesis, but what I've hoped to indicate here is that successful parish models are usually designed to fit the parish needs rather than conform to a particular model. In the most viable and enduring programs, we find identifiable parts of many of the models. The successful parish, it seems, not only chooses what best meets its needs, thereby constructing its own unique model, but it also offers a variety of models for sub-groups. For example, in some of our best parish models of family ministry, we find a peer group model, some clusters, and a family home evening. Each of the last two might touch only a dozen families, but it's there for them.

For some of the above material, I am indebted to Sandra DeGidio, OSM.

7 Further Areas of Consideration and Recommendation

There are some gray areas in the field of family cate-chesis that need to be mentioned. These are sometimes uncomfortable to address in the diocesan office or parish because they involve personnel relationships, budget, and the like, but they are so crucial to effective family ministry that it would be remiss of me to omit reference to them.

Clarification of the role of family in the parish religious education structure A corollary of this is the relationship between family-centered and formal religious education classes. We find many parishes that set up family programs without discussing underlying philosophy, ramifications of a successful program, and allocation of parish resources. The first question a parish needs to discuss is: Do we envision our family as a support to the parish and its programs, or do we envision the parish and its programs as a support to the family? This is more than mere word play. It is germinal to the whole concept of family ministry. If the pastoral staff, parish council, and board of education truly view as their goal the revitalization of a strong faith *within the family,* then efforts and resources will be directed first toward that goal. If, however, they give it verbal primacy while continuing to allocate resources and personnel toward programs *within the parish,* they are subtly telling parents that they are convinced neither of the parents' primacy nor of their competency in becoming the first and foremost faith nourishers of their children.

I am reminded of an instance of this on the national level. In preparation for the Synod of Bishops on Catechesis, a symposium was held on the Catechesis of Children and Youth in Marriottsville, Maryland, in March of 1977. One of the general papers invited, and the one to which I was invited to respond, was on the Catholic family. The author fell into the very common practice of ignoring the family to talk about adolescents and schools; the author effectively blocked out, once again, any discussion of Church responsibility to the family in its own milieu. This paper was delivered before a most august group of Catholic religious educators, yet the vision of family ministry stood light years behind the vision of sacramental, parish, and adolescent ministry.

If the diocese or parish views renewed family faith as its first goal, then all of its educational efforts should be designed with this goal in mind, whether they take place in a total family context, a weekly instruction for children setting, or the parish school. A CCD school or parish school that does not engage and inflame family faith at home remains child- and subject-centered, not family-centered. If a parish plans to operate three systems of catechesis—through the family, through CCD, and through the parish school—it must create new ways of involving the family at home *through* these systems. It might almost be said that the first purpose of these schools is to enrich the faith climate at home. As a minimum, it must let parents know that the enrollment of their children in the classroom-religion system presumes that they are actively interested in becoming more, not less, vital faith nourishers themselves. It follows that these parents can be expected to pledge themselves to prayer and spirituality efforts at home, to attend parenting and renewal of faith classes themselves, and to take an active part in planning, teaching, and ministering to other families in areas in which they are competent. These efforts toward family involvement will begin to eliminate those parents who feel they have fulfilled their responsibility to their children and to the parish by enrolling them in the school or CCD and by paying tuition. But its real value is to the family itself. It will utilize the very educational systems that sometimes take on parental responsibility to revitalize the first faith community, the home. In this way, the parish can come to grips with the familiar dilemma of espousing family-centered faith while continuing to spend its time and resources on subject- and child-centered instruction.

Acceptance of a plurality of family styles worthy of ministry
Even a cursory reading of the needs requested by the people of God of their Church indicates that the parish needs to look hard at its catechetical ministry to those not usually counted

in the nuclear parish family—the divorced, the single parent, the widowed, the couple whose children have grown up and gone away, the youth, the committed single, the interfaith couple. Yet, in a depressing reading of the recent *National Inventory of Parish Catechetical Programs,* we read that 30 percent of our parishes never offer marriage preparation, 60 percent never offer parenthood, 74 percent never offer ministry to the divorced or separated, 55 percent never offer marriage and family enrichment, 71 percent never offer natural family planning, 73 percent never offer family living and sex education, 54 percent never offer programs for senior citizens, and an astounding 81 percent never offer programs for singles. Parish youth programs are nearly as discouraging when one realizes that of services offered youth, the most common is organized sports. Three-fourths of the parishes admitted never having scripture-study courses for youth, an area where youth are most interested and are flocking to groups outside the parish for such study and community.[25]

Allocation of time to study, reflect upon, and design programs   When Bishop Stafford introduced the Pastoral Plan of Family Ministry to the American bishops, he said that he could not in conscience recommend adoption of the Plan if the bishops were unwilling to allocate resources for more staff on the national level. This same kind of reasoning needs to be applied on the diocesan and parish level. We cannot expect present diocesan directors and DREs, who are in many cases already overloaded with programs and ministries, to begin to meet the voids in ministry mentioned above without additional time and assistance. Each parish must look at its own situation.

As one means to achieving the time necessary to reflect upon total family and parish ministry, I commend those parishes who are suspending formal religious instruction for one year in order to focus upon the needs of its families and to develop programs to meet those needs. This is especially appropriate in preparing for the Year of the Family. Other parishes are adding or developing personnel to meet new ministries. Diocesan directors are expected to help train personnel, and they, too, need time to develop training programs. One of the hallmarks of good family ministry is that it is carefully studied, considered, and designed before it is implemented. We have too many examples of failure where overworked pastors and DREs grasped at a program and experimented with it before they or the parish were ready.

A parish might begin by examining its underlying philosophy on catechesis and then prioritizing programs, staff, and budget accordingly. Sabbaticals should be considered for staff who need further study on the sociology, psychology, and spirituality of the family today. The total family minister was one professional who was considered in the early stages of the Pastoral Plan of Family Ministry but who seems to have become lost in drafts along the way. We envisioned this new professional as more than a family DRE. He or she would be trained in developing family spirituality and in skills such as communication, counseling, sexuality education, and parenting education. This is still a valid goal in our quest toward full family ministry. Without additional skills, many religious educators cannot address larger family needs.

Some parishes are beginning to grant sabbaticals to staff to acquire these skills. Others are seeking DREs who have already taken courses in marriage counseling and family communication. This author recommends that diocesan directors encourage DREs to broaden their summer update studies of the traditional theology workshops and courses to include courses on chemical dependency, social ministry, communication, parenting, counseling, and sexuality education. These will not only give the DRE new dimensions to his or her own ministry, but it will ultimately give the parish more foundation in family ministry.

Pastoral vision and cooperation   There is a subtle attitude found on the part of staffs in many parishes that parents don't care about the religious life of their children. This usually stems from lack of parental interest in adult education programs and family workshops offered. It also comes from hearing too often the familiar parental questions: "When are you going to? . . ." and "Why don't they? . . ."

We must constantly remind ourselves that while we see parents as primary faith givers, their background in an earlier Church conditioned them to believe that only Father, Sister, or the classroom could really teach their children religion (which, in their thinking, was synonymous with faith). The major fault of these parents is that they believed what they were taught. Simply because we have a vision, and admittedly some data, proving their centrality to their children's eventual adult faith, does not mean that they share that vision or even believe us.

Many of the adults in the pews are suspended in adolescence. They look to Father for reaction and approval. It is regrettable but necessary that in many instances the pastor must lead them through this adolescence by giving parishioners a full understanding and his approval of new forms of ministry before they will accept it from other staff professionals. This, of course, implies pastoral education. That there is a clear need for renewed pastoral education on the family was emphasized by the Papal Committee for the Family in its paper, "The Family in the Pastoral Activity of the Church." Two passages need to be mentioned here:

> The bishops realize that a serious preparation should be given to priests and religious as educators of the family. In various countries the bishops are aware of the difficulties encountered by priests in presenting and promoting the objectives and evangelical ideals of marriage and family life. One comes to realize that if families do not always know what course of action to follow, it is because they are often left in uncertainty by their spiritual guides. The crisis that is being experienced in the priesthood can be linked with the crisis known by many families: a renewed priesthood will save the family, and vice-versa.
>
> One notes overall an awareness of the need to prepare priests in a serious manner for this pastoral ministry in the service of the family. Too often priests are formed in seminaries for a ministry to individuals, independently of their social milieu. It is necessary to help priests to be more attentive to the family as a social unit, and to the place of each of its members in the evangelical renewal of the family as the first milieu of life.[26]

Pastoral vision and enthusiasm are so essential to effective family catechesis that it is linked with the key indicator of success—shared staff vision. Yet pastoral indifference, lack of reading, updating, and familiarity with family catechesis remain a serious block in many parishes and dioceses. If the bishops are sincere about revitalizing family faith, it seems they must begin with the revitalization of the parish family faith-nourisher—the pastor and other clergy. Until they are familiar with the theology and rationale behind family catechesis, many of our efforts will not bear fruit.

Integrating parish ministries One of the features of effective family catechesis is that it affects and is affected by other parish ministries. Paricularly helpful is the existence of a strong parish social-action ministry. The vitality becomes cyclic: the stronger the family program, the more it evidences itself outward in ministry to others. This strengthens the social ministry which, in turn, attracts more families. Rosemary Haughton alluded to this in her paper at the Atlanta hearing:

> Contrary to popular belief, the best marriages and the happiest families don't happen because people concentrate, first of all, on the quality of their relationships, but rather when the couple and then the family as a whole is involved in something bigger. . . . Of course, it isn't necessarily a conscious religious dedication. It can be some kind of social work or concern. . . .[27]

Let me cite a homely example of involving families in parish social outreach. One parish with which I am familiar began a simple program of asking families to prepare lunches to take on Sunday to the "hotel people," those elderly who live in residential hotels in downtown areas where restaurants are closed from Saturday evening until Sunday morning. Whole families make sandwiches, pack lunches, and take turns delivering them to the elderly, who are as hungry for human contact as they are for food. This simple effort has given numerous families a renewed sense of family faith, a sense of parish community, and a dedication to others. What the project has done for the elderly is insignificant compared to what it has done for families themselves.

Youth ministry, liturgical ministry, social ministry, and educational ministry all impact family ministry. A strong family catechetical program does not detract from but rather strengthens other parish ministries.

Envisioning the healthy family as minister   Tolstoy begins
Anna Karenina with prophetic words, "All happy families
resemble one another; every unhappy family is unhappy in its
own fashion." Family sociologists and theologians alike are
calling for family ministry developed from the strengths
rather than from the pain and pathology of families. Our
family ministry of the past was often after the fact: we coun-
seled hurting families rather than developed strong healthy
families. Dr. William McCready wrote of this in a paper
commissioned by the USCC:

> For a long time such programs have dealt with impaired
> families which have been so defined. Usually it is deemed
> necesary to delineate the "problems" and "needs" of such
> families in order to develop responsive programs. There is
> no question that problems and needs exist, but so do healthy
> families who are coping with problems of all kinds. Why do
> we not spent some resources to discover how families are
> able to do as well as they are instead of constantly focusing
> on the pathology of families? It is likely that we would learn
> a great deal that would be useful to ministers and pastors in
> the field as well as to troubled families.[28]

In our pews, we are often aware of parents, elderly, and
singles who have strengths and successful experiences which
they can share with others. In my work in family spirituality,
one of the first questions I ask of the pastor or DRE is,
"Who are your mustard-seed families?" They always know
who they are. These are the ones to tap, not to stand before
large crowds in the parish and lecture, but to quietly offer
help to other families who are seeking renewed prayer and
spirituality. Often, the effectiveness of the family DRE
depends upon his or her ability to coordinate the experienced
and the needy in family ministry whether it's parent-teen
relationships, like-to-like ministry with the single parent, or
young-mother ministry.

I would like to quote here from one unsigned diocesan
director's survey sheet because it is perceptive and exciting.

> The Church or parish can be a place where parents get the
> opportunity to talk with one another. Church officials, not
> being parents, are limited in giving advice to parents. Parents
> and children need conversation, cooperation, and consolation

from other families. Church or parish is one of the few agencies for creating that opportunity.

The Church can be a resource center for family education. People, literature, and services should be available. Family education programs have to be aware of people who are not in families but are part of the context of families. Usually, senior citizens are untapped resources.[29]

8 Signs of Hope in Family Catechesis

I have tried to be as realistic as possible in presenting reality and vision in the field of family catechesis. One of the questions I can anticipate after a workshop with professionals in the Church is the simple one, "Are you hopeful about the future of the family in our Church?"

I am more hopeful now than I was ten years ago, when I was idealistic and unrealistic in expecting parishes to meet needs that they hadn't yet perceived. These family needs are now articulated and obvious. Our bishops have not only validated the idea of family ministry but have authorized a vision and a strategy. Granted, a majority of our parishes have never offered parenting courses, family spirituality enrichment, support for fragmented and broken families, interfaith families, or other forms of family ministry (excepting eucharistic preparation for children), but those statistics represent parish ministry prior to recent family efforts in the larger Church.

More promising is the growing number of parishes which are serving as models of family ministry for other parishes around the country. In 1979, I was asked to write the text for *Models of Ministry: Family Life Resources for the Parish,* a book describing thirty parishes where family ministry makes a difference.[30] Commissioned and published by the United States Catholic Conference Commission on Marriage and Family Life, this magazine-size book went into every rectory in the United States. In studying the research on parishes presented me, I was encouraged by the number who are sincerely trying to expand from a strictly educational concept of parish into a broader caring faith community concept. Briefly, here are some of the programs I described.

- In St. Andrew's Parish, Fort Worth, Texas, we found married couples training engaged couples in marriage preparation, taking the load off the pastor and giving couples the benefit of the lived experience of marriage. The pastoral team uses its time to train the married couples, who are put through a rigorous program, and also to support and affirm them once they begin their ministry to young couples.

- Our Lady of Lourdes Parish in Altoona, Pennsylvania, found that not all of its couples' needs were being met by Marriage Encounter, so it took steps to furnish two marriage enrichment groups, one for those encountered, one for those who were not. Pastor and couples want the two-prong couples' program to continue, because they have found that the more couples benefit from a renewed marriage, the more the parish benefits.

- In White Bear Lake, Minnesota, St. Mary's Parish has a once-a-month program for single parents which has expanded to embrace a simultaneous program for the children of the divorced. During these sessions participants talk about their situations, hurts, and relationships with children/parents. "This needs to be done over and over," stresses the coordinator, "until the hurt isn't so bad anymore."

- Visitation Parish in Kansas City, Missouri, has a viable program in which the elderly of the parish are adopted by families who see that they remain an integral part of parish and family life.

- In St. Theresa's Parish, Phoenix, Arizona, there's an active program of widow-to-widow ministry in which widows are matched up with the more recently widowed. They work through the grief process together, do things together, and in many cases, become good friends.

- Successful family catechesis programs were found all over the country, but we chose St. Albert's of suburban Madison, Wisconsin as the model to describe, because it involved close to half the parish families in its program. Similar successful models to study are: Church of the Resurrection, Tulsa; St. Mary's, Colorado Springs; Blessed Sacrament, Madison; St. Michael's, Detroit; Holy Trinity, Denver; Good Shepherd, Cincinnati; and the Marine Corps Base, Camp Pendleton, California.

- In North Dakota, we discovered a pastoral team making a great effort to listen to the needs of the Indians at Standing Rock Indian Reservation. "It is our goal to discover more deeply the spiritual, social, and psychological needs of our people," said the pastor. "Where better can this be found than from the people themselves?" Two priests and two sisters with background in theology and psychology travel the reservation and visit the homes of the people to hear their needs.

- St. James Parish in Miami, Florida, is a good example of a parish where leadership develops leadership among the laity. An Encountered couple took over as family life directors in the parish, and within a short time, they have involved numerous other laity in the day-to-day ministry of families.

- The divorced and separated gain strength from each other in an active program at St. John the Baptist Parish in Peabody, Massachusetts.

- Special needs of the young marrieds, as contrasted with the usual parish couples' groups, are met by couples themselves in St. John Francis Regis Parish of Kansas City, Missouri.

- *Welcome to the Widowed* is a program that deals with loneliness, lost sense of purpose, alienation from the parish community, and grief among the widowed at St. Columban's of Birmingham, Michigan.

- St. Michael's in Olympia, Washington, has developed an active social-action program involving a great number of volunteers who are ready to step in and help others in need, be it hungry people, hurting families, or others in crisis.

- We found a program of ministry to the very young at Good Shepherd Parish in Cincinnati. The goal is to provide an opportunity for parents of infants, ages four and under, to get together to share ideas, fears, hopes, strengths, and weaknesses in order to get the support they need while guiding their children through these impressionable years.

- St. Peter's Parish in Spokane holds an annual parish dream session to hear the needs of its people and set goals for the parish community. As a result of one such session, one staff member said, "We are careful not to overschedule events, taking families away from their homes. Events scheduled center on simple ways families can deal with sacraments, prayer, personal development, and so on."

- Older singles are ministered to by one another in a program at Holy Apostles Parish in Colorado Springs, Colorado.

- A rural parish in northern Wisconsin has developed its own unique program of marriage preparation because the others available did not meet the needs of its parishioners. Holy Rosary Parish in Medford, Wisconsin brings in resource people to discuss subjects like problem solving and communication: "Where is all the money going?"; Church requirements and law; prayer, God and sharing; and human sexuality.

- *Groups* of parishes combine family ministry efforts in Chicago in the Northwest Divorced Catholic Group. And in St. Paul-Minneapolis Archdiocese, Deanery Four ministers to beginning families. This inter-parish effort holds immense potential for the churches of the future.

- Four parishes were chosen as outstanding models of total family ministry, that is, parishes that do not have just one or two programs meeting the needs of specific families, but parishes that have attempted successfully to meet the needs of all their families. In each of the following parishes, we found programs involving a high percentage of laity as ministers and we noted that the success of each family-ministry effort promoted another expansion into a new area of family need. Just as one need was being met in these parishes, another was perceived. Certain hallmarks are present in all four parishes: shared pastoral-team vision, involvement of the laity, ongoing educational, spiritual, and emotional support of lay ministers, a sense of ownership of the parish by all, meaningful liturgies, and the development of a sense of parish as a family that cares about one another.

These four parishes include St. James, Arlington Heights, Illinois; St. Timothy's and St. Joseph's in suburban Minneapolis, and St. Thomas More in Tulsa, Oklahoma. All are worth visiting if readers are in the vicinity.

As author of the *Models of Ministry* resource, I was struck by a recurring fact: practically all of these programs and the others we studied were initiated by coordinators of religious education in the parish who saw a need outside the strictly educational sphere and met it. If there are unsung heroes in the development of our eventual family ministry efforts, I am convinced they will be the directors of religious education in the parish (a role commonly played by pastors as well as religious and laity), because it is they who are listening and piloting the needs in these models of ministry. It is they who give us hope in scanning the future of the family in the parish.

Finally, certain trends became evident as we continued to study the successful models. These were by no means authenticated other than being common threads that seemed to run through parishes with viable programs of family ministry. Here they are.

1. Good total family ministry seems to flow from successful family-centered catechesis. All four of our models of total family ministry began with several years of family-centered catechesis. It's fair to say, we believe, that once the parish gets involved in family programs (as opposed to catechesis for children only), it realizes the prior needs in families and rises to meet them. Many of the best programs in ministering to the needs of the divorced, for example, came from family-centered catechesis and the realization that single parents have special needs.

2. Sadly, we did not find one viable model of ministry to the interfaith marrieds; yet, these comprise nearly 50 percent of our marriages nationally. We asked and asked, but the only help interfaith marriages seem to be getting is in form of a few classes before marriage, yet the problems arise after marriage.

3. We found little ministry to the families of drug and alcohol-using offspring. Yet, in a 1978 Gallup poll of Catholic families, this kind of counseling headed the list of needs that parents want met by their Church.

4. We suspect that an increase in professionalism on the staff of a parish does not decrease the need for volunteers. In the many parishes that have hired Masters of Social Work or professional marriage and family counselors, the leap in volunteerism is dramatic. We wonder—is it that when parishioners sense professional leadership today, they are more willing to serve?

5. Lack of participation of men—singles, fathers, husbands— in family ministry programs was mentioned only twice. Could it be that ministry to couples might be the spur to lead traditionally apathetic men into action?

6. Most of our successful models are in suburban, white, middle-class parishes.

7. Most of our successful models are in the Midwest. All four of our total family ministry parishes are in the Midwest. Both coasts (with the exception of the Pacific Northwest) and the South had the fewest models. The Southwest had several.

8. When the bishop has a clear vision of family ministry, it shows through the diocese.

9. Where there was one good model, there were usually two: Fort Worth, Kansas City (Missouri), Minneapolis, Phoenix, Miami, Chicago, and Colorado Springs. Why? Does it mean that a working model nearby gives another parish the courage to try it? Or is it competing? We don't know, but there were too many coincidences to dismiss geographical similarities.

10. Once a parish implements a family ministry program, it is more open to implementing another. The major step seems to be initiating the first program. After that, the doors open to ministry to all kinds of people: widows, older singles, children of divorced.

These were some of the trends that appeared. Since we didn't study those parishes without any family ministry, we cannot claim comparison data. Still, the above observations may be of some value to parishes now considering taking a step into family ministry.

Ministry to the family will take time to sift down from the bishops, the USCC, papers like this one, and the many excellent family workshops now offering leadership. More pastors are becoming educated to family ministry. Among professional religious educators, the concept of family catechesis is being broadened to include the total family environment within the total parish family structure. We are utilizing authorities and studies on the family from many disciplines—psychology, sociology, education—to flesh out our theology. We are becoming more interested in the faith of the family than in the religious instruction of the children. We have a timetable and a challenge to meet the needs of the family holistically and catechetically in the decade of the 80s.

There is hope that we can do so, but not assurance. Our success will depend on our own faith, not only in the Trinity, but in the sureness of our vision and in our perseverence in working toward achievement of this oldest but newest form of ministry—the family.